EARTH
BREATHS

Words by **Oshri**

Art by Andrea Ceballos García

BUTTERFLYON BOOKS

Earth Breaths
Written by Oshri Liron Hakak, illustrated by Andrea Ceballos García

Published by Butterflyon Books
Los Angeles
ISBN 979-8-9868755-0-7

For Mama Earth

Even those of us who live surrounded
by concrete are made of soil.

We don't have to look
any number of generations back to see
that all of our origins
are a rich blackish brown and beautiful.

A paradise of a planet calls out under the madness of our frenzied toil...

If you keep going like this,
my ancient riches are bound to spoil!

5

Through the plants of my soil I give you the air
so you can breathe and laugh-
do you feel my deep care?

Creatures of all kinds enjoy my great fare,
from snails, frogs and sparrows,
to the panda bear!

But the way you humans are going
is a slippery slope of a snare.
And at this rate soon you'll lack the wood
to make even a chair.

I don't want to fill you with even more stress-
au contraire!

13

Rather I'd like us some
earth breaths to share.

15

After all, separating EARTH and BREATH
is but a B...
and I'm calling and counting on you
to find a new way to BE.

17

This has been my gift to you...
in your stillness,
in the fullness of your lungs,
in the beat of your heart,
all of my melodies and rhythms
live in each of you,
as you are made of my air, water and soil.

Breathe in the sanity of my peace,

21

Breathe out the turmoil.

23

Breathe in your knowing
that you are my precious child,

25

Breathe out the need to compete
with your brothers and sisters.

Breathe in the confidence
that we must heal together.

Breathe out the worry
that you must face my crisis alone.

Breathe in the truth that you are part
of my billions-year-old life story.

Breathe out the idea
that you have ever fallen short of anything.

35

Please, Love, take some earth breaths today...
of all you have to do do do,
it's the one thing I ask of you not to delay.

37

Hearing Mama Earth's ask,
let's fill ourselves up,
drinking her air as from a healing tea cup.

39

Her trees breathing into us
and we into them,
A great togetherness here,
now is when.

41

THE MEND

43

45

Resources

Here are some organizations working to help Mother Earth that you can get involved with:

Save Soil
https://consciousplanet.org/

Ecosystem Restoration Camps and Communities
https://ecosystemrestorationcamps.org/

Replant the Forest Festival
https://www.replanttheforest.org/

Kiss the Ground
https://kisstheground.com/

The Nature Conservancy
https://nature.org

Sierra Club
https://sierraclub.org

Keep in Touch

You can find the creators of this book on Instagram -

Andrea Ceballos García at @andreakushisha
Oshri Hakak at @oshrihakak

More titles by Butterflyon Books:
ButterflyonBooks.com

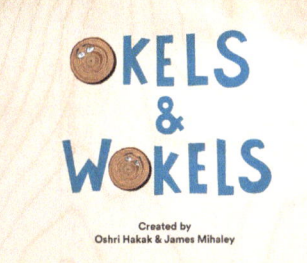

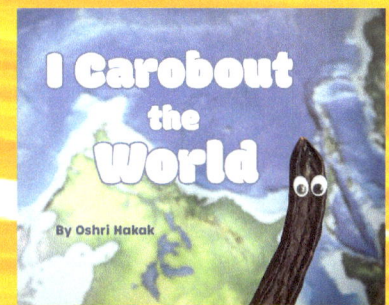

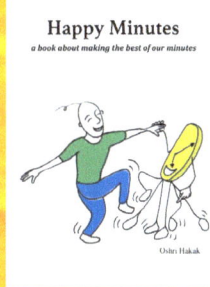